NEW SAT™

2016 VOCABULARY

Copyright © 2015 Blythe Grossberg, Psy.D.

How to Use this Book

The new SAT™, to be released in March 2016, is a
redesigned test intended to measure students' readiness for college in
new ways. Instead of asking students to define words in isolation,
the new test asks them to understand words in the context of
passages that represent a range of difficulty. One passage is drawn
from a U.S. founding document (such as the *Declaration of
Independence*), and another text addresses a topic such as justice
(from a speech by Martin Luther King, Jr. or another author). In
addition, test-takers have to find the parts of texts that serve as
evidence for a point, and they have to define words, including their
specific shades of meaning, in the context of a passage. Other
sections of the new SAT™ ask students to revise a text and to

correct grammatical mistakes or rhetorical questions, and the optional essay section asks students to analyze a passage. Finally, the math section asks students to solve math problems and analyze data. There is a greater emphasis on data analysis in the context of other fields, including science and social science, as well as on Algebra and on solving equations.

These sections call on students' knowledge of what is called "Tier Two" vocabulary—those words that appear across domains or subjects and that are of an advanced nature. Tier One words, on the other hand, are simpler words that people usually understand through conversations, while Tier Three words are those that are specialized to a subject or domain and rarely occur outside of that domain (for example, medical words).

This guide concentrates on familiarizing test-takers with Tier Two vocabulary words that students need to understand to perform well on the SAT™. While there is no certainty which words will appear on the SAT™, a familiarity with these words will help a student on the test by allowing him or her to read more fluidly and accurately. Some of these words also apply to the math section. Each

word is defined in simple rather than complicated terms so that most

students can understand it, and, as most of the words on the new

SAT™ must be defined in context, the word is also shown in the

context of a sentence or short passage.

While this is not the only book that students need to prepare

for the new SAT™, it will help them decode the vocabulary on the

test so that they can understand and answer the questions.

How to Learn Vocabulary

The key to learning new words is to see them in the context of a sentence or passage. After you look over this list, try to find these words in the passages you read in books, the newspaper, and magazines. You are more likely to find them in high-quality fiction, non-fiction, and what are called primary source documents (historical documents that are originals). If you find other words you don't know when reading, jot them down and look up their meaning or meanings. As you look up the definitions of words, keep in mind that a word can have several different meanings, and the SAT™ will ask you to define the meaning of a word in context (meaning the way it is used in that passage). If you look up unfamiliar vocabulary words regularly, you'll find that you are suddenly seeing and hearing them everywhere. This type of reading is the best way to prepare for taking standardized tests and for college.

Word Lists

Words Related to Analyzing Passages:

* **analogy**: a comparison between two things, usually made to clarify one of the things. For example, you could use reasoning by analogy to compare a bird and a plane, as they both use wings to fly.

claims: the position the author is taking; in other words, the argument the author is making. Claims can also be a verb, as in, "The author claims that…".

concision: refers to an author's ability to convey or express an idea fully with relatively few words. In general, concision is valued in many types of persuasive writing.

conclusions: what you can draw from the passage; in other words, what are the main ideas the author arrives at after presenting his or her evidence.

confirm: to back up the truth of something that has already been said. For example, some passages will confirm an earlier passage or statement.

contradict: to go against an argument; to state the opposite of an argument. For example, some questions will ask if one passage within a text contradicts another.

conventional (language): follows traditional or generally used forms. For example, a conventional love poem often uses words of praise.

counterclaim: the argument that refutes or goes against the claim. For example, if the author is claiming that a law is fair, the counterclaim would be that the law is unfair.

diction (elevated diction): the choice of words in writing. Elevated diction, for example, involves choosing sophisticated and perhaps unfamiliar words.

discipline knowledge: Understanding of a certain field of knowledge, such as a knowledge of physics or psychology. The word "discipline" refers to training people to follow standards or codes of behavior, but it also means a branch of study.

explicit meaning: the clearly defined meaning, not what is suggested or implied.

Application: Some passages will ask you the explicit meaning of a text, that is, what is directly stated or described in the text. For example, the poem "O Captain! My Captain" by Walt Whitman is explicitly about a ship captain, meaning that idea is what is directly referred to in the poem.

- **figurative language**: language that is not strictly or literally true and that often includes metaphors or similes, which are defined in this list.

- **focus**: what the author concentrates on. The focus of a persuasive essay, for example, is what the author is trying to convince readers to accept or agree to.

- **idiom**: an expression with a meaning that is different than what the words it contains expresses literally. For example, the idiom "hold your horses" means to wait, but it does not necessarily (or even likely) mean that you hold back horses.

- **implicit meaning**: The meaning that is implied but not clearly or directly expressed. It is different from the explicit meaning. Some passages might ask you about the implicit meaning of a text, meaning what is suggested by it but is not in it. For example, the poem "O Captain! My Captain" by Walt Whitman, the implicit meaning of the poem is its reference to the death of Abraham Lincoln, the captain of the country.

- **infer/inference**: to infer or to make an inference is to conclude something based on the evidence you are given. For example, if a person has chills and a temperature, you can infer that he or she is sick. In reading a passage, you make have to draw conclusions about what the author thinks or feels based on what is stated in the passage. For example, if the author makes many negative comments about a political figure, you can infer that he or she is not in favor of the politician's policies or ideas.

- **language precision**: refers to how exact or precise the author's language is. For example, is the author vague or confusing, or does he or she define terms and ideas clearly?

metaphor: an expression that involves a comparison between things that aren't strictly or literally true. For example, the metaphor "her movements were those of a snail" mean that the person was slow but that she wasn't actually a snail. Figurative language involves using metaphors and similes (see below).

point of view: the author's or narrator's position on a topic, or the perspective from which he or she writes. For example, a story can be written from the point of view of a character or a narrator.

purpose: the reason the passage was written. For example, is the passage intended to entertain people, convince them of an argument, dispel (get rid of) a misconception, etc.

reasoning: the method or way in which the author makes or defends his or her point. For example, if the author is contending or stating that slavery is wrong, how does he or she defend or support that point?

- **sequence:** the order of a passage. For example, in which order does the author make his or her arguments?

- **simile**: is a comparison that uses the words "like" or "as." (A metaphor, in contrast, does not use "like" or "as.") For example, "she was as hungry as a wolf" is a simile. Similes are used in figurative language.

- **structure**: refers to the way in which a passage is organized. For example, does the text start with the main idea and move on to details?

- **style**: The way in which a passage or piece of writing is composed or written. For example, some pieces are written in a journalistic style (resembling a piece of reporting that might appear in a magazine or newspaper or online news site), while others are more poetic.

- **support**: refers to the evidence in a passage that backs up an argument or claim. For example, you may have to find the part or details of an argument that an author uses to back up his or her claim.

• **syntax**: The way in which the author arranges words in a sentence.

• **textual evidence**: support that comes from the text. For example, if a question asks you for textual evidence, you want to locate (and possibly quote) part of the text that supports or relates to that point. Some evidence can be stylistic, that is it relies on the author's choice of words, while other evidence can rely on an appeal to the reader's emotions, ethics (moral principles), or reason.

• **themes, or central ideas**: are the main or recurring (meaning frequently appearing) ideas or thoughts in a text.

• **Tone**: The author's tone refers to the general character or attitude of a piece of writing; the author creates the tone by choosing specific words. For example, an author can choose poetic words (those often used in poetry to evoke a mood or scene), argumentative words, angry words, etc.

- **transitions**: Changes in a passage from one section or idea to another. Often, transitions are marked by words such as "in addition," "also," "in contrast," etc. These words can help the reader understand the relationships between ideas. Often, transitions are marked by new paragraphs or, in the case of poetry, stanzas.

- **word choice**: refers to the specific words an author uses and how they affect his or her meaning. For example, does the author use sophisticated or simple words, does he or she repeat words, etc.?

Words Related to Historical Documents

- **Abolitionism**: a movement to end slavery; in the United States, the movement largely in the 1800s that concentrated on ending the slave trade and slavery before and during the Civil War. The word comes from "to abolish," meaning to get rid of something.

- **amendment (to the Constitution)**: a change to the original document. Twenty-seven amendments have been added to the Constitution since its ratification.

- **appeal**: to make a request for a higher court to hear a case that was already tried in a lower court. Usually, people who make an appeal are hoping to reverse the decision of the lower court (meaning that the higher court will decide in the opposite way to the lower court). Appellate courts have jurisdiction, meaning the right to try cases, that deal with appeals.

- **appropriation**: An amount of money used for a specific purpose. For example, a legislature can make an appropriation for building a bridge.

- **article**: an article can often refer to a paragraph or section of the Constitution or another document. Another meaning of the word is a piece of writing that appears in a newspaper or magazine.

- **Bill of Rights**: the first ten amendments to the Constitution; these include the rights of freedom of speech, assembly, religion, to bear arms, and the protection against unreasonable searches, among other rights.

- **bipartisan**: involving the cooperation of two political parties that don't usually work together. When bipartisan cooperation occurs, it is called bipartisanship. The opposite is partisan (see below).

- **campaign finance**: the way in which campaigns for public office and for the passage of laws are paid for. Many laws have attempted to reform, or change, the way campaigns are paid for.

civil: this word has many meanings. In a legal sense, it refers to the rights of citizens. Civil rights refer to the rights of citizens; in the United States, the Civil Rights movement was the movement by to ensure that all citizens, including African-Americans and all other citizens, had the rights, such as the right to vote and right to a fair trial, that are given in the Constitution. There are two main types of court cases in the United States: civil and criminal. Civil cases involve one party (such as a corporation or government) suing another party (such as an individual or another corporation) for not carrying out their responsibilities. The other types of cases are criminal cases.

Confederation, confederacy: a confederacy refers to several units working together in a political union. In American history, the term can refer to the Articles of Confederation, which governed the country during and after the American Revolution (from 1781-1788) and to the Confederacy of Southern states that formed an unrecognized alliance to secede from the United States during the Civil War (1861-1865). A confederation involves states working together, for the most part largely independently, while a federation, such as the United States government, has a stronger central (or federal) government.

Congress: the part of the federal government that passes laws. It has two parts: the House of Representatives and the Senate, so it is bicameral (meaning it has two chambers).

Constitution: the document that established the way in which the government of the U.S. would be run. Since it became law in 1789, 27 amendments (or additions) have been made to it.

convict/conviction: as a verb, to convict means to declare someone guilty of a crime. It is usually done by a jury but sometimes by a judge.

criminal (charges): a person charged of a crime is charged in a criminal court. A person accused of violating federal law is tried in a federal court, while a person accused of breaking a state law is tried in a state court. If a person is convicted of a crime, or determined to

18

be guilty of that crime, he or she will receive prison time, supervision by legal authorities, or a monetary penalty (or all three of these penalties).

executive: The executive branch of the government includes the President and the related agencies he or she runs. The executive branch is responsible for carrying out the law.

factions: in the early years of the Republic, factions were political groups. James Madison described factions in the *Federalist Papers*, a series of essays arguing in favor of the ratification of the U.S. Constitution, as groups that pursued their own interests over the importance of promoting the greater good (what's good for most people or for the whole). Madison believed that a republic created by the Constitution would be able to protect the country against factions.

federal: one of the meanings of federal refers to the central government in Washington, D.C., as opposed to state, city, or local governments.

felony: A crime more serious than a misdemeanor and generally punished more severely in a court of law.

framers: a term for the Founding Fathers, the people who fought against Great Britain in the American Revolution and, more particularly, helped write and ratify the Declaration of Independence and Constitution.

high crimes: The phrase "high crimes and misdemeanors" appears in the U.S. Constitution, and it refers to crimes carried out by public officials who have a responsibility to serve the public and follow laws that come from their office. A "high crime" can only be carried out by someone in a public office who has taken an oath to follow certain laws.

impeachment: refers to the process of accusing an official of wrongdoing. The process can result in the removal of the official from office as well as in criminal or civil charges. According to the Constitution, the president can be impeached by the House of

Representatives (similar to an indictment in a criminal court), meaning that the House thinks there is enough evidence to go forward with a trial. The Senate then decides whether or not to convict, or state that the president is guilty of the charges brought against him or her. The Senate must convict by a two-thirds majority, and if the President is convicted, he or she is removed from office.

indictment: a formal charge against someone in a criminal court. A person is said to have been indicted.

interest groups: interest groups are organizations that promote particular causes. The term is very broad and can refer to charities, civil rights organizations, corporations, trade associations, and other groups. Sometimes interest groups, also called advocacy groups, engage in lobbying the government, meaning they try to persuade the government to pass laws favorable to the group. People who lobby are called lobbyists.

judicial: the judicial branch of the government refers to the court system. The other branches are the legislative, or law-making branch (the Congress on the federal level), and the executive branch (the President and related offices). The members of the executive and legislative branches are elected by the people, while members of the Supreme Court, the highest court in the country, are chosen by the President and confirmed by the Senate. The judicial system refers to the entire system of federal and state courts.

jurisdiction: refers to the power to make decisions. For example, a court may have jurisdiction over a certain area, such as a state, so it can try cases in that area. Some courts also have jurisdiction over certain types of cases. For example, the Supreme Court has original jurisdiction, or the right to try a case when it is initiated, in cases that involves disputes between two states, among other types of cases.

jury: a group (usually of 12 people) that hears evidence and makes a verdict, or decision, in a court of law. Jurors (those who serve on a jury) are supposed to be impartial and reach a verdict based only on the evidence presented to them.

legislature/legislative: The legislative branch of the government is responsible for making or changing laws. On the federal level, it includes the Congress, which is bicameral (has two houses, the House of Representatives and the Senate).

misdemeanors: crimes less serious than felonies. Perpetrators of misdemeanors are usually punished less severely than people who commit felonies.

null, nullify: To nullify a law means to make it legally void, meaning that people do not need to follow it. In several crises before the Civil War (and during the Civil Rights era in the 20th century), states nullified federal laws, stating (incorrectly) that they did not need to follow them. However, the Constitution says that states must follow federal law.

parties (political): In the United States, there have generally been two main political parties at any given time. Now these parties are known as the Democrats and the Republicans. There have been different party systems in the United States (which have included other parties) in history. Today, most politicians belong to one of the two main parties, though others are Independents and members of what are called third parties.

partisan: as an adjective, partisan means supported by one political party or group. The opposite is bipartisan, which means that opposing parties have cooperated to produce a law or proposal.

progressive: attempting social change or reform. For example, a progressive politician might want to change or improve laws or social conditions.

ratification, or ratify: To ratify is to give consent or agreement to something. For example, a proportion of the states in existence at the time had to ratify the U.S. Constitution in order for the document to become law.

reform: to make changes, often in a political or social institution, to improve it. There have been many reform movements in U.S.

history, such as the movement to reform prisons or to abolish slavery.

secession: the act of withdrawing from a political union or federation. In the United States, secession usually refers to the withdrawal of 11 Southern states from the union during the Civil War.

tax reform: the effort to change the way taxes are collected by the federal government. Some tax reform movements in U.S. history have attempted to reduce the amount of taxes people pay, while others have sought to make tax collection more progressive (meaning that people with different income levels pay different amounts or percentages of their income).

treason: the crime of working against one's country, for example to overthrow the leader. The Constitution defines treason as helping the country's enemies or waging war against the country.

Vocabulary Related to Math

acute: an acute angle is less than 90 degrees.

adjacent: adjacent angles share a side and a vertex (corner point) but don't overlap. A side that is adjacent to an angle is next to it.

average: the average is the same as the mean; it is calculated by adding up all the scores in a data set and dividing them by the number of items in that set. It is different than the median and the mode.

bisector: a line that cuts an angle or line into two equal parts.

concave: having an outline that curves inward. Concave polygons have one or more internal angles that are greater than 180 degrees, unlike convex polygons. A star is concave.

congruent: congruent angles or shapes have the same size. Congruent values are equal.

constant: A constant in math means a number that does not vary or change. For example, in the equation $x + 5 = 9$, 5 and 9 are constants, while x is the variable (it can vary or change).

converse: in math, the converse involves switching around the "if" and "then" parts of a statement. For example, "If it rains, then I will bring my umbrella" is the original statement. The "if" part is the hypothesis, and the "then" part is the conclusion. To make the converse, you switch the "if" and the "then." The converse would be, "If I bring my umbrella, then it will rain." These statements have very different meanings.

convex: means extending outward. Convex polygons have no internal angles that are greater than 180 degrees, unlike concave polygons. For example, a rectangle is convex.

difference: the answer to a subtraction problem. The difference of 10 and 2 is 8.

exterior angle: the angle between any side of a shape and a line extended from the next side.

equilateral: an equilateral triangle has three equal sides and three equal angles (each 60 degrees).

functions: relationships in math in which the number that is put into the relationship only results in one value as an output. In other words, each x or value you put into the equation results in only one value, or one y. When graphed, functions must pass the vertical line test; that is, a vertical line drawn anywhere on the graph must pass through only one point. If it passes through more than one point, such as through a circle, the graph does not represent a function. Functions are often written as f(x), pronounced "f of x."

hypotenuse: the longest side of a right triangle; it is the side opposite the right (or 90 degree) angle.

inequality: an equation with a greater than (>) or greater than or equal (≥) to or less than (<) or less than or equal to (≤) symbol.

interior angle: the angle inside a shape. The interior angles of a triangle add up to 180 degrees, and the interior angles of a quadrilateral or four-sided shape add up to 360 degrees.

inverse: an inverse function reverses a function. For example, if a function maps an x to a y, the inverse maps the y to an x. To find the inverse of a function, replace the x with y and the y with x. The inverse is noted as f^{-1}.

isosceles: an isosceles triangle has at least two sides that are the same length. In isosceles triangles, the base angles (opposite the equal sides) are also equal.

legs: the legs of a right triangle (one with a 90 degree angle) are the two shorter sides. The legs both have acute, meaning they are less than 90 degrees.

line of best fit: is the line on a scatter plot with data points that best represents the data points. To find the line, you can use a graphing calculator or choose two points on the line, find the slope of the line between them, and write an equation for this line.

linear equation: an equation that defines a straight line. An example is $y = 4x + 2$.

median: the number in the middle of a data set arranged in numerical order. In other words, half the numbers are greater and half are lesser. In a data set with an even number of items, the median is the average of the two middle numbers. The median can be different from the mode and mean. The median of the data set 2, 5, 6, 8, 9 is 6.

mode: the most commonly occurring number in a data set. In the set 2, 4, 5, 5, 5, 6, the mode is 5.

obtuse: an angle that is more 90 degrees and less than 180 degrees.

possible solution: a solution that satisfies an equation. It may be only one of many values that can satisfy that equation (in other words, you can put in the value and it makes the equation true).

product: the answer to a multiplication problem. The product of 6 and 4 is 24.

quantitative: data that represents numbers, as opposed to qualitative data, which are data that are not numbers.

quotient: the answer to a division problem. The quotient of 20 and 10 is 2.

random: a number that is chosen at random is chosen in a process in which every number in a data set has an equal chance of being chosen. For example, winning lottery numbers are chosen in a random way.

regular: Regular polygons have sides and angles of equal length and measure. For example, in a regular pentagon, all five sides have the same length, and each angle has the same measurement in degrees.

scatterplot: a graph for data that plots the *x* values on the horizontal axis and the *y* values on the *y* axis. The *x* value is usually the value that is put into an equation, while the *y* value is the output or what comes out of the equation.

similar: two shapes are similar if their only difference is size. Their angles are the same, while their sides are in a common ratio to each other. For example, one triangle can be similar to another triangle in which each side is twice as long but the angles are the same.

sum: the answer to an addition problem. The sum of 6 and 2 is 8.

system of equations: two or more equations for which the solution works for all the equations. The equations can be linear (defining a line) or non-linear.

transformation: a transformation of a function changes the graph of the function. For example, adding a constant to the *y* value of a function moves it up or down.

valid: true. A valid solution is one that works for an equation.

_xy_ plane: the plane formed by the x and y axes.

yield: in a math problem, yields means provides a solution. For example, $10 - 2$ yields 8.

Made in the USA
Middletown, DE
29 June 2015